Old UDDINGSTON

by
Rhona Wilson

Laurelbank, Main Street. c.1904

ISBN 1 872074 90 1

Main Street, Uddingston

Introduction

The first reference to Uddingston appears on the Ragman's Roll of landowners who swore allegiance to Edward I in the thirteenth century. 'Walter, son of Rodger of Odiston' illustrates one version of the name which fluctuated wildly between Ediston, Odingstonne and others, before arriving at the more familiar corruption of Udinston in the early eighteenth century. Various scholars have broken up the name throughout the years in an attempt to offer an explanation of its origins, all of which have been given a sceptical thumbs down by present day language experts. According to the School of Scottish Studies the most that can be assured is that 'Udd' probably refers to an Anglian name such as Ada or Oda, dating it to some time after 1000 AD.

As a tiny settlement with a population of only 280 by the late 1700s, Uddingston didn't merit its own feudal lords in earlier times and made do with Bothwell's instead. David I gifted this larger village to David de Oliford who is thought to have built a wooden castle somewhere in the vicinity. Bothwell Castle proper - with its original entrance from Uddingston - was built by Walter Murray in the thirteenth century when he acquired the lands through marriage. The castle took a battering in various skirmishes with the English but by the 1360s it had been restored under the reign of the infamous Archibald the Grim. After marrying into the Murrays this powerful lord brought a relative degree of peace to the surrounding districts, Uddingston included.

Weaving and farming were Uddingston's staple earners in the eighteenth century. There were eighty hand-looms in the village at one point and several arable farms producing crops such as wheat, oats, pease and beans. With communications less than perfect the isolated villagers had to be reasonably self-sufficient and other occupations lint growing, work at the tannery or at the malt kiln. In 1811 Uddingston's weavers were involved in a strike and This included harmful competition from power-looms such as the nearby Blantyre Mill eventually dried up the supply of work. For a time there wasn't much to turn to apart from local foundries like Wilkie's plough work (which revolutionised ploughing internationally) or nearby stone quarries.

New technology brought coal-mining and a new lease of life to the village in the mid-nineteenth century. Coal could be accessed at much greater depths than previously and the village expanded as industry developed. Between the 1830s and '60s the population doubled, arriving at 1,300 in 1867. If employment couldn't be found in Uddingston itself, there was work in the surrounding areas; many men crossed the river to work at Blantyreferme Pit and the nearby brickworks.

Around the pits satellite villages such as Tannochside and Thorniewood sprung up to provide housing for the 'incomer' miners, and by the early 1880s the population had expanded again - due in part to Irish immigrants attracted by the work - to around 3,500. Although a huge increase, it was modest compared to surrounding areas at Motherwell or Bellshill. Uddingston's chances of major expansion were thwarted its sandy soil which couldn't support heavy machinery.

However, services and communications developed as Uddingston grew. The railway arrived in the late 1840s to service the surrounding coal fields. A private gas company was in town by the 1850s with street lighting appearing by 1862. Previously supplied by wells, Uddingston's local water supply became inadequate as the village expanded and a gravitational water supply was acquired in the 1880s. Despite this, the initial building boom, to accommodate miners and those profiting from the industrial revolution, dropped away between 1860 and 1905 and in the first fifty years of the twentieth century there was a noticeable lack of new housing. Uddingston had to wait until the 1960s for council schemes to be built.

After the coal mines were exhausted, Uddingston, like most of Lanarkshire, tells the same sorry story. The reliance on mining had not allowed for the development of replacement industries and a new era of light industry, factory employment and travelling to find work emerged. Although Caterpillar and Tunnocks both built factories in the sixties, the M74 bypass arrived in the same decade and took the main route to London - formerly down Uddingston Main Street - with it.

Despite the closure of its pits, the village was until the late 1970s considered as grim, grey and industrial and definitely on the unfashionable side of Glasgow. Many of the buildings were blackened and damaged by years of exposure to factory smoke belching over them. Strange then that 'yuppification' in the 1980s transformed Uddingston into a rival to such well-to-do places as Bearsden, Milngavie and Newton Mearns. This was largely due to private house building geared towards the top end of the market and Uddingston continues today as a fully-fledged dormitory town, full of new inhabitants who sleep there but work and play elsewhere.

OVER 40 ADVERTISING HOARDINGS in **UDDINGSTON, BOTHWELL, BELLSHILL, and MOSSEND.   Lists sent on application.**

These ad boards are a tad more sophisticated than earlier adverts used by Uddingston merchants. Thomas Tunnock's first ads in the Uddingston Standard went no further than a belligerent 'Pie Tam' in big letters.

The Old Town, Uddingston.

In the 1790s the Old Town was the only area of Uddingston which had any buildings at all and most of these have long gone with the exception of Easter Farm just in picture on the left. The original Easter Farm was at the corner of Old Mill Road and Spindlehowe Road, and later became Pollock Farm but Farmer Ford took the old name with him when he moved to the site here.

Clydeneuk House, built in the late 1850s, was better known to locals as the Candyman's Castle after its one-time owner John Poynter who may have had connections with Halton's, the local confectionery manufacturer. Candyman Poynter had his own private zoo which had its pros and cons for Uddingston locals. Watching monkeys scampering along the retaining wall was novel to say the least but listening to hyenas screeching through the night was infuriating. His savage watch dogs weren't particularly popular either and some messenger boys refused to go past the gates. Poynter died in the 1890s leaving his fortune to one Rebecca Edgar, subsequently rumoured to be his illegitimate daughter, but she died a few years later having managed to spend a fair proportion of her inheritance. All that remains of the mock-baronial mansion today is its ornamental fountain.

Cross & Bellshill Road, Uddingston.

The block on the left is still known as Simpson's Corner after its owner who ran a florists and fruit shop there, famed for its loose sherberts which were sold by weight from big glass jars. To the right of Bellshill Road, reaching out into Main Street, the tenement blocks and the sweetie shop have long since been replaced by new housing, grass and trees. The Royal Bar, just at the right of the picture, has moved round the corner. A tenement row, called the Lindams, was once situated behind Bellshill Road its name derived from the smelly Lint Dams. These were shallow pools used in the flax-producing days of the eighteenth century for soaking lint fibres and the smell they gave off was apparently atrocious. The tenements were demolished in the early 1970s.

This section of Bellshill Road held a fair number of small stores . Stark's Grocer was at No.20 with the Starks themselves living next door. Further down on the left of this picture was another grocer which obtained its stock from local supermarkets and, unsurprisingly, didn't last very long. On the right-hand corner was an Italian cafe patronised for its gigantic, barrel-shaped water ices. Much of this area was affected by development in the 1960s and 70s with the cottages on the left being demolished to make way for Tunnocks factory.

Uddingston Cross was the venue for social gatherings and political meetings such as those held by the suffragettes, who were causing annoyance to local men in 1914 by their campaign of ringing the few people who had phones and screaming 'Votes for Women!' before hanging up. Even today, the Cross is used as a meeting point for a depressingly young group of men. All the buildings on the immediate right of this side of the cross have gone. The Royal Buildings on the left are still standing with a new selection of shops on the ground floor and Friel's Solicitors at the corner.

The presence of Tunnocks pervades Uddingston. The factory, vans, teacakes - who could miss them? This picture shows 'Pie Tam' Tunnock outside his first shop in Bellshill Road. In 1890 his business began in a rather more humble fashion, selling pies and scones from a wash-house near his home. Around the start of the First World War he moved again to Loanhead Terrace, where the tearooms are today. Thomas died a couple of years later and the business was run by his wife until his son Archie returned from the forces. At the end of the Second World War they had around a dozen employees and this has since become thousands, employed within the massive Tunnock factory built almost opposite the original shop in the sixties. That shop, along with Donald's butcher and the McCallum dairy next door, have all long disappeared.

Tunnocks Factory today dominates the left-hand side of this view of Bellshill Road, replacing many tenements and taking up quite a large section of the village. New buildings which have appeared within the factory vicinity are the pebble-dashed Church of Nazarene and the Job Centre. The Anvil Inn appears just past Simpson's Corner, set back from the line of buildings seen here and the corner building itself is now home to the McKenna bookies. To its left is a building originally the home of a Mr and Mrs Lang. At the moment it is boarded up, having failed to wow the natives as a 'Honey Pot' cafe - a plywood Winnie the Pooh is still outside offering a balloon to Main Street. The Tunnock family plan to set this building up as a museum of their company and of Uddingston, but work on it is yet to begin.

MAIN STREET, UDDINGSTON.

Uddingston Main Street was formerly the main route south and has had to put up with varying forms of traffic throughout the years and until the M74 bypass opened, the village was subjected to a constant stream of heavy goods lorries heaving through the village en route to London. Trams arrived in Uddingston's vicinity in 1903 as Lanarkshire Tramway cars passed through on the way to Motherwell. Despite protests by some that the trams would bring in unwanted crowds at the weekends and otherwise take away business away from the village, Uddingston got a more extensive service four years later which was as popular as anywhere else, judging by the hoards of customers in this c.1920 picture. However, private bus companies began to come to the fore in the 1920s and the tramways slowly died out. The last Lanarkshire tram left Uddingston in the early thirties, although the Glasgow Tramway Company soldiered on until 1948. When the tram tracks were finally removed the last sett was built into a pillar in the entrance of the Tunnock factory.

The changing traffic situation of the 1940s is well in evidence here as cars and trams jostle for space. By this time the Lanarkshire Tramways had gone along with its tram tracks; the tram in background belonged to the Glasgow company. Trams died out as the bus operators of the twenties improved their facilities and varied routes to suit their customers, and after they were gone the bus company's started to fight for custom amongst themselves. In a fierce rivalry, Hunter and Frame buses picked up and dropped off customers anywhere and everywhere in their race for customers - in fact two of their bus drivers once came to blows in Main Street. On the left-hand corner is Bailie Barr's tenement which once held Barr's sweetie shop .

LOANHEAD MANSIONS, MAIN STREET, UDDINGSTON

Loanhead Mansions were built in the early 1900s and named after Loanhead Farm which Main Street sliced through. The old Post Office building can be seen in the middle at the back (the unofficial PO used to be at a grocer shop run by Andrew Jackson in the Porterswell area). Around the time this picture was taken entertainment in Uddingston consisted of football, travelling circuses and talking. Old editions of the Uddingston Standard tell of dancing bears visiting Main Street and the community of those days spent a lot of time hanging around outside, and watching the sights for fun.

In Forrest's Map of 1816 Uddingston had no Main Street, no Glasgow Road, no railway and no villas. Main Street arrived around 1826 as part of Telford's reconstruction of the Carlisle-Glasgow Road, taking a route through grasslands such as Loanhead Farm. Going through such land that was clear of obstructions meant that the road took a wider and straighter direction than most Main Streets. Locals called it the New Turnpike Road with Glasgow Road being designated as 'Old'. The top picture shows an unsurfaced Main Sreet, still the domain of the horse and cart. The occupier of the first shop around this area was the owner of a model railway who installed it as his sole attraction. Customers were charged one penny to look at it until Ross the chemist moved in.

Uddingston's first commercial properties were built in Main Street around the middle of the nineteenth century. William Barr built the tenement block at the corner of Bellshill Road and Main Street with flats above the shop units. The Horse-shoe Bar was beside it with Loanhead House next to that, later replaced by Loanhead Mansions. About halfway along there was a temperance hotel. The corner at the right-hand of this picture used to be known as Gow's Corner because of Gow's Grocer at Church Street. When Main Street was built both Church Street and Spindlehowe Road were excavated to match its level, creating the West and East Cuts.

Just down from the Cross at Old Glasgow Road lies the sparse remains of the Loancroft Estate. Loancroft House was built in 1835 by the Cross family, on lands previously known as Bakershill. In 1915 it was bought by Thomas Prentice, an Uddingston grocer who made his real money breeding hackney horses, that time's equivalent of the Rolls Royce. After the First World War his son started a successful poultry farm which was leased out as a going concern during the next war. By the thirties the family no longer lived in the big house and this was rented out to the Taylors and Quinns, amongst others. After the Second World War, the poultry farm was set up again on a small scale which didn't survive amongst the competing battery farms of the time. The family decided to sell off the land and by 1960 Loancroft Gardens housing scheme stood in its place.

Loancroft Poultry Farm. Uddingston.

Loancroft Poultry Farm. The last portion of Loancroft ground was sold in the eighties to Balfour Beatty who developed the area around Loancroft Gate, the original site of the mansion house. Today all that remains of the estate is a red sandstone cottage, just round from the housing schemes, and formerly the estate's servant's quarters. One half of this cottage was previously used as a hackney store and the building presently used as a shed still has horse stalls inside. Jim Prentice, grandson of Thomas, lives in the cottage and his garden's magnificent mature trees give a hint of what the estate was formerly like.

By the 1950s Main Street looked a lot sprucer. Few houses had been built in Uddingston since the Second World War and by this time problems of overcrowded, poor housing began to be felt; indeed, in the late fifties tenements in Kirk Street and Church Street had been abandoned by their owners and paying tenants. Those willing (or forced) to live in such squalor could do so for free and if you were lucky enough to find the means to leave you simply sold the keys. Conditions such as these led to a petition for council housing and the first three-storey council flats finally appeared in Uddingston in 1961, the first since the twenties.

Uddingston's first railway station was opened in 1849 as part of the Clydesdale Junction Railway, later taken over by the Caledonian Railway. The population was only around 470 at this time and a fair proportion of that was made up of navvies employed for the railway. In the early 1880s the railway station was still isolated from the village and surrounded by farms but these disappeared as the coal-fields expanded. Development was such that by the turn of the century there were two more stations, run by the North British Railway. For both Caledonian and North British, coal was the most important cargo and passengers were looked upon as a bonus. They competed fiercely with each other on journey lengths and frequency of service and eventually the Caledonian Railway won out.

In 1914 Jack Riley caused an accident at the Caledonian Railway station. Desperate to catch a train leaving the station, he flung himself onto its outside, closely followed by the outraged station porter. Neither had chosen the wisest course of action and Mr Riley was rushed to hospital by horse ambulance with broken ribs and a crushed back.

In the late 1890s the entrance to what is now Crofthead Street was a narrow lane past the old slaughter house, formerly Hornal's engineering works. The tenement blocks on the right were threatened with demolition but survived as the council developed its conservationist policy. In the fifties and sixties the idea of renovating and modernising Victorian buildings hadn't occured to local councils and buildings such as these were happily got rid of. Perhaps that's what happened to the tenements near the Cut at the back , which have all gone, replaced by low-level housing and a small park. Also gone, Crofthead Street's George Cinema, in the 1940s the owner was fined for not showing the statutory quota of British films - his audience preferred Hollywood.

Dominie Smith set up Uddingston's first gas supplies in the form of a private company in the 1850s. Common in the nineteenth century, coal gas works involved heating coal until it gave off gas and this was used to power amenities such as streetlighting, which Uddingston had by the 1860s. Overall the service was taken up slowly in the town because, although it was cleaner and more convenient some landlords refused to install it due to the initial costs involved. There were also several accidents through ignorance or misuse and some Uddingston homes were still burning paraffin even in the 1960s.

The gas Works entry office, 1989. The works were one of almost two hundred taken over to form the Scottish Gas Board in the late 1940s as part of the nationalised industry. After this production lasted for less than twenty years, although the two gasholders remained on site to supply gas during peak demand periods until the 1980s. The first holder was demolished in 1985 and the last was taken down ten years later to make way for a Gateway supermarket.

Before the new mill was built at Calderpark this road to the old mill was known as Mill or Miln Road. The tenement to the left is the back of Wises' garage known previously as Jack's Land after the old landowners. 'Wee Ireland' was situated between Old Mill Road and Spindlehow Road, this name going back to the mid-nineteenth century when the area was favoured by Uddingston's Irish immigrants. John Wilkie, inventor of the revolutionary iron plough, lived in this area in the early nineteenth century. 'Wilkie's Plough' made ploughing much more efficient and proved a successful export; one commentator of the day remarked without irony that "demand for Wilkie's plough in the West Indies has greatly increased since the emancipation of the slaves."

These sorry-looking buildings, pictured left, are the back of Sydney Place in 1973. The space in the middle of the shot was at one time the site of the Cross toilets. In the 1970s the houses were under a demolition order and the tube at the front of the picture is actually one of many metal bollards put up to stop people parking their cars. Pictured right, the old tenements were pulled down a couple of years later and eventually replaced by new flats.

The buildings on the right of this 1901 view of Old Mill Road were demolished in the sixties to make way for the massive Tunnocks factory. Renovation was an unknown word in the sixties and most of the town's Victorian and Edwardian housing was damp and decrepit with no modern facilities. Many were privately owned and easily demolished before the days of compulsory purchase by the council. There were a few grumbles about Tunnock's new building taking up such a large site near the centre of town but, really, the old-fashioned smoke-blackened tenements razed to allow space for it were unwanted. By the late seventies, however, conservation was becoming an issue to contend with and the resulting U-turn in council policy allowed Rosslyn and Joadja Place to survive. Another survivor was the cottage on the left corner, once a stable and coal store, and presently the site of the Church of Nazarene.

By 1964 Tunnocks new factory, seen here under construction, was producing a mammoth 4,000 pies a week which gives some idea of the size of the operation. The factory is huge but, as factories go, not the ugliest I've seen and most Uddingston inhabitants seem to feel the same way. Tunnocks' profile within the town is high to say the least - casual conversations about something else entirely always seem to squeeze in a reference to the company or to the family. Throughout the first half of the twentieth century Tunnocks was curiously untroubled by strikes when strikes were standard and its predominantly female workforce seems to have found conditions better there than in other industries within the area. The people of Uddingston appear to have a genuine regard for a family which have provide much needed employment over the last century.

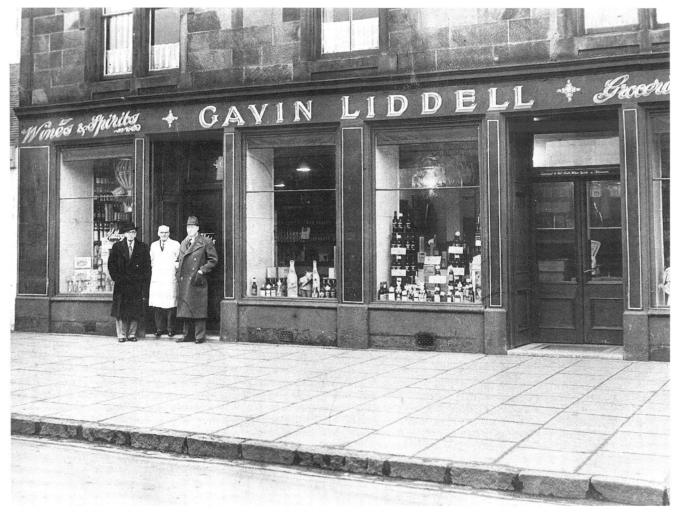

Boyd Tunnock and Gavin Liddell appear in this picture, along with one of the grocer's shop assistants. Liddells was one of the two shops originally at the front of Tunnock's first factory building in Old Mill Road. The factory went up in phases, this tenement block disappearing at a later stage in its development. Originally, there was also a cobblers shop next door but Liddells had expanded to take over its premises around the thirties or forties. Hughie Green, a famous Uddingston cricketer, lived in one of the flats above the shop.

This 1902 picture makes for a startling comparison with present day Clydeford Drive. The single row of houses here have been joined by countless more over the years, replacing the fields and nursery with a tight network of homes.

Communally owned co-operative shops date back to the end of the Napoleonic Wars when they sprung up in industrial areas hit by post-war recession. The annual dividend was the main advantage of shopping there. This could amount to as much as ten weeks wages - a huge amount - and was a great help to families on a low income. Uddingston Co-op was built in 1891 and has now been reborn as a Scot-Mid supermarket. The adjacent tenement block has been demolished and replaced with a new road leading to private parking space for new flats.

Uddingston Cricket Club was formed in 1883 and its first matches were played at Woodhead Farm in Birkenshaw before they moved to the castle policies. The club won the Western Union Championship from 1899 to 1904 inclusive - an impressive run even if there were only six teams in the league at this point. Recent decades haven't been so kind to the club. In fact chroniclers were still citing 1906 as a good year even in the seventies! The new pavilion seen here was opened in 1910 and replaced in the 1950s. After war was declared in 1939 the cricket club grounds were requisitioned for use by the army (as a leisure facility?) and one day members found themselves locked out of the grounds. After some intense negotiations they were eventually allowed to clear out their lockers but they weren't allowed to play again until March the following year. The pitch and pavilion were released although the army kept the rest of the lands - perhaps they fancied some entertainment.

UDDINGSTON BOWLING GREEN.

Uddingston Bowling Club was established in the 1860s on ground at the local gas works but this c.1906 shot was taken at the present site on the Old Glasgow Road. Football teams were also proliferating in Uddingston by the 1870s. At the turn of the century virtually every street had its own team although many of these amateur clubs only lasted a year or two. It was an Uddingston footballer, in fact, who had the dubious honour of initiating the penalty kick in the 1880s. John Hendry, playing for Nottingham County later in his career fisted a ball clear of the goal. There was such a furore that the rules of international football, drawn up by the British, were changed for evermore.

Haltons Confectionery Works at Spindlehowe Road, responsible for the wonderful Sherbert Fountain, fell victim to an arson attack in 1914. This was the main industry in Uddingston after coal mining and hundreds of employees were left jobless. The destruction was complete as the burning roof had caved in on the highly flammable materials, causing an internal furnace which destroyed the entire stock and machinery. It was discovered afterwards that the works' offices had been subject to a burglary attempt and it appeared that arson was the revenge of thwarted thieves. Some sight seers made the best of the situation, however, as police were sent to nearby tenements the day after to search for stolen toffee! Two miners were jailed for the crime and the works were rebuilt, only to be brought down again by the bulldozers a few decades later.

Maxwell Place and Joadja Place on Spindlehowe Road around 1904. George Watson, the investor who financed it, named Joadja Place after a Joadja Creek in Camden Colony, New South Wales. The word is made up from the first two letters of three Christian names - probably those of the first settlers there - and Watson brought the name with him when he returned to Uddingston from Australia in 1890. Nearby was a curling pond which was lit by huge kerosene lamps when used for skating on winter nights.

POWBURN TOLL, UDDINGSTON.

Demolished in 1973, Powburn Toll was positioned at a junction in the nineteenth century to dissuade turnpike travellers from sneaking past without paying. Turnpike roads were controlled by cartels, usually of local landowners, who maintained the roads in return for the toll charge. In fact maintenance was low and the schemes were little more than a licence to print money by those who had more than enough anyway. Tolls were abolished in 1878 and Uddingston's old toll house became the town's first police staion until new premises were built in Bothwell Road in 1924. Around 1913, Pat Breslin, heavyweight boxing champion, was arrested at the toll after he fired a pistol during a fight between crowds of his supporters. He was later released and a complimentary concert was held in Uddingston Public Halls by a forgiving public eager to help him out with any expenses incurred. The bridge now to the right of the toll house achieved notoriety as one of the first 'box girder bridges' which required substantial repairs.

VILLAS AT UDDINGSTON

29999 JV

This turn of the century view of the area just down from the Toll has changed dramatically. The villas, housing Uddingston's better off inhabitants, initially looked onto the grasslands but the lovely M74 motorway now cuts right through the bottom of this picture. Construction began in 1966 and was completed two years later. Although the motorway also sliced through Main Street one local writer commented that there were certain advantages since it separated Uddingston from the veritable Calcuttas of Glasgow, Tannochside and Bellshill.

An atmospheric inter-war view of Bothwell Road, with these two ladies more than likely heading off to the shops on Main Street. Shopping in those days and even as late as the sixties and seventies, was a job in itself. Queuing for ten minutes at the butchers, followed by queuing at the grocer's, then the bakers, and then it was on to the next shop, for more queuing, queuing, queuing.

Watson Street, c.1924.

Lizzie's Sweetie Shop was on the corner of Muiredge Street, opposite Muiredge Primary School. This picture was taken in 1973 after it had ceased trading.

The back doors of Muiredge Street in the same year. By this time the life of the street was coming to an end eviction notices had been posted on the back doors; demolition followed in 1975.

TANNOCHSIDE HOUSE.
BIRTH-PLACE OF JAMES HOZIER M.P. GRAND MASTER MASON SCOTLAND.
BRANDON SERIES.

Tannochside House was built near the Calder in the early seventeenth century and was also known as St. Enoch's Hall. This latter name harks back to Lanarkshire's ancient connections with St. Mungo, the Christian settler. St Enoch is a corruption of the name of his mother, St Thenaw, although it is unlikely that she was ever in Uddingston itself. The first owners of the house included old land-owning families such as the Jacks and the Raes. At the time of this 1904 picture it belonged to the Hoziers, relatives of Winston Churchill's wife. James Hozier, MP for South Lanarkshire and Grand Mason Master, was born here in 1851. Like so many country homes, Tannochside House was eventually deserted by its owner and it was only a mater of time before the industrial bemolition.

Tannochside and Thorniewood began to develop 'up the hill' around the 1880s when Uddingston's population was burgeoning with the influx of Irish and Ayrshire miners. Hozier Street and Cuthbert Street began life as cheaply built miners rows around 1870. In the late 1880s Tannochside Colliery went into production with two pits on the Hozier estate run by the Monklands Coal Company. Some miner's wages were paid out at the Brusher's Bar - I wonder if the Hoziers owned it! With its entire economy based on mining, Tannochside was inevitably doomed as the pits were worked out and by the late 1920s miners rows were being demolished. A few decades later old Tannochside disappeared as new industries, such as the huge Caterpillar factory, were erected in the fifties and sixties.

Facilities appeared in Tannochside as its small mining community took root. Asides from Tannochside School, there was a cinema of sorts, known as the 'Puggie' because it looked like a colliery pug shed. This burned down and was never rebuilt but the site was taken by a Miners Welfare Institute some years later. Over the years Tannochside, along with anywhere else 'up the hill', seems to have acquired a fearsome reputation in the village. In 1958 Uddingston Ratepayers' Committee tried to block the council's plan to create an industrial zone near the town. Factory employees would of course come from 'up the hill' since there was 'no unemployment in the village' and as there was plenty of room 'up there' for factories it was suggested that building them in Tannochside would be to the inhabitants' advantage since 'the employees would have less to walk'! Various articles in the Uddingston Standard also looked on the bright side of families being decanted 'up the hill', commenting that the council had wisely chosen to move the least desirable members of the village community.

Thorniewood tells much the same story as Tannochside. Nackerty (also known as Aitkenhead) was the nearest pit with tenements, such as those pictured here c.1910, built for its miners. Like anywhere else the works suffered their share of strikes although, by contrast, 700 men found themselves locked out by United Collieries in 1914 in retaliation for a complaint to the regulatory body regarding tonnage rates. Coal was also often paid by the 'hutch' system which meant that the whole truckload was forfeited if it didn't fall within a certain narrow weight band. Miners were faced with many disadvantages in their work place, not least the constant danger of explosions, and although coal companies often provided houses this meant that a family's home could be lost if a man lost his job or died. Isolated pit communities also often had just one general store, usually run by the coal company who charged extortionate prices and offered all too tempting credit to workers with several mouths to feed.

The fate of Daldowie has been an unusual one. Before the fourteenth century, Calderpark and bits of Daldowie belonged to Newbattle Abbey. The monks were removed during the Reformation, after which the lands of the two estates passed to the Stewarts of Minto. Financial difficulties, the bane of many a posh family, led to them giving up their properties in the mid-seventeenth century. Daldowie House was built by the estate's eighteenth century owner Robert Bogle and was rebuilt and extended throughout the following century. The last owner of note was John Dixon of the Calder Iron Works who lived there in the 1820s. Today, the site of the mansion house has been taken by Daldowie Crematorium, built in the mid-1950s.

At the same time as they lost Daldowie, the Stewarts also had to give up Calderpark Estate. James McNair, a Glasgow sugar refiner and investor, built the villa here in the early 1800s on a feu from Daldowie lands. Further change appeared in the mid-1870s when the North British railway line was laid through the lands but this was a mere hint of the spectacular changes to come in the twentieth century. After Calderpark's last occupiers, the cattle-dealing Websters of Baillieston, had moved out the mansion house was left to the usual Lanarkshire fate of subsidence, neglect and demolition but a stay of execution was given in the late thirties when the estate was bought by the Glasgow and West of Scotland Zoological Society with a view to establishing a permanent animal exhibition.

Crushingly, the conversion of the country estate into Calderpark Zoo was delayed for ten years, mostly due to the Second World War. It wasn't until 1947 that Calderpark Zoo was ready for visitors but even then its enclosures consisted only of speedily assembled second-hand building materials. Regardless, the forties were great for the zoo, and huge attendances were drawn by stars such as Margaret Lockwood taking part in the publicity drive. However, financial difficulties have been the problem ever since. A cheque from a Glasgow businessman, Herbert Ross, paid off a huge overdraft in the fifties and during this decade the zoo approached Glasgow Corporation more than once to transfer it to a more accessible site. Despite this, new buildings and animals arrived throughout the sixties. In the nineties zoos have a much harder time justifying their existence but Calderpark has survived, these days placing great emphasis on conservation and education.

In the run up to the zoo's opening in 1947 the Hamilton Advertiser was full of excited stories about the various penguins, wallabies and lions still in transit, bound for the zoo, as if - really - they might not make it. Glasgow suburbs had better watch out - their streets could be full of wild, detouring beasts hungry for a snack. At this time, though, the zoo's white peacock was considered its most exotic exhibit. The animals here were pictured around 1950 and it must be said that the image of an elephant wandering happily through the trees seems idealistic to say the least. Over the years some animals have become more equal than others with a chosen few, such as good old 'Jimmy' here, earning a public name. This culminated in the nineties with the madness of the celebrity polar bear. Winston Polar, happy being just another bear previously, became the city's weather barometer, courtesy of Radio Clyde's 'eye in the sky' slot. Captain George daily informed the public of Winston's movements (if he was in his hut - rain; gambolling happily - sun) and even after his demise Winston's old enclosure remained, somewhat ridiculously, empty as a Mecca for his fans.

The Viaduct. Broomhouse.

Spectacular change has affected this landscape since this picture of 1906. A 1914 Ordnance Survey map shows the viaduct on the North British line positioned just down past Calderpark Zoo entrance and Old Roundknowe Road. This line was built through the estate in the mid-1870s and probably transported freight from the nearby Broomhouse Colliery, the viaduct crossing the North Calder water. Today, viaduct, railway line and colliery have all been consumed by a vast motorway network. Just down past signs for the Redstones Hotel at the beginning of the A721 there is a red sandstone bridge, about three or four times as wide as the crossing here, which I estimate to be the site of the original viaduct. If you look in the same direction as the photograph - towards the Daldowie Crematorium - you will notice the arched bridge in the background has been swapped for a concrete, square type and is also carrying its own motorway.

Hamilton Road, Broomhouse

Hamilton Road, passing through Uddingston, Hamilton and Broomhouse was the main Glasgow to London stagecoach route. Like the Rowantree Inn near Tunnock's factory, the Old Coach Inn served travellers on the coach and the horses were changed here. Turnpike or drove routes were often a principal reason for an area developing as they allowed the means for goods and people to come and go. Still standing today, the Inn was rundown for many years until the development of the motorways gave it a new lease of life; both the building and its menu have since been upgraded to cater for the new breed of car-owning travellers. With a conservatory attached to the gable-end and expensive furnishings throughout, the atmosphere is definitely family orientated - no doubt locals prefer the sparser pub across the street. The background of this view from the turn of the century now features a pedestrian bridge spanning the road.

Looking in the opposite direction, this picture shows the view across from the Old Coach Inn around 1917. Trams had long replaced the stage coach and the road shows signs of much needed improvement. Both the Scott Memorial Hall and the cottage-type dwelling beside it have gone although some dwellings slightly further up the street remain. The two-storey tenement block, in particular, is still with us and couldn't fail to be noticed as it is currently painted a lurid Mediterranean orange. At the moment, new building is being carried out on this section of Hamilton Road and an empty space full of debris occupies the spot next door to the Memorial Hall. The turnoff to the Old Coach Inn appears at the foreground on the left.

Broomhouse P.O., a mere hut in this 1906 shot, indicates the size of the community at the time. The house to which it was attached can be spotted in the previous picture of Hamilton Road, just before the tenement building. This rather pitiful post office was replaced in the first instance by a new one a little further down the street.

Scott Memorial Hall, Broomhouse.

Lanarkshire's Memorial Halls just go to show that if you want to be remembered don't bother hall one. Various buildings sprung up in the county throughout the late nineteenth and early twentieth centuries, but with enough cash to maintain them. As a result, many of these dilapidated buildings are now being demolished. The Scott Memorial Hall, however, met its death by burning some five years ago. A new block of housing is currently being built in its place.

BIBLIOGRAPHY

First Statistical Account
Second Statistical Account
Third Statistical Account
Hamilton Advertiser
Uddingston Standard

Henderson and Waddell, *By Bothwell Banks*, D. Hobbs & Co, 1904
Jamieson, David, *Uddingston the Village Parts One, Two, Three, Four & Five*
Jamieson, David, *Uddingston in Old Picture Postcards*, European Library, 1984
McPhillips, John, *Doon the Hill - Up the Hill*, Scottish & Universal Newspapers Ltd, 1976
Simpson, W. Douglas, *Bothwell Castle*, HMSO, 1978
Stenlake, Richard, *Bygone Uddingston*, Stenlake & McCourt, 1989